Alice in
Wanderland

Alice in Wanderland

Alice Randt

authorHOUSE®

AuthorHouse™
1663 Liberty Drive
Bloomington, IN 47403
www.authorhouse.com
Phone: 1-800-839-8640

First published by AuthorHouse   04/27/2011

ISBN: 978-1-4567-6437-1 (sc)
ISBN: 978-1-4567-6436-4 (ebk)

Library of Congress Control Number: 2011906498

Printed in the United States of America

To You, the Readers

*A*lice in Wanderland is the result of twenty-two years of motor coach travel. Because of this, I've created a magic box full of stories about these travels, and now I'm passing some of them on to you. People are funny! Everyone is unique! Some are more unique than others. That is what makes tour managing so enjoyable.

I thought it only fair not to use real names, except for the drivers; if they didn't object, I used their real first names. If I wasn't sure, I changed their names. The stories are as true as I can make them. Just so you know, I remember the incident but not the person involved.

By reading this book, you will realize that as long as there are men, women, and outhouses on this earth, there will be stories to tell. The truth is that as long as people take motor coach tours, the stories will grow, flourish, and spread. What I feel most after working for Rustad Tours (in my opinion, the best company) is gratitude—gratitude for giving me the opportunity of doing what I enjoyed and getting paid for it.

Chapter 1

I have to tell you about this guy named Don; I told him he is getting his own chapter because he is so unique. I think he should come along on every tour just for amusement. Don is a very nice fellow; he doesn't get into trouble on purpose—things just happen to him.

On a beautiful fall day in October, our coach pulled into the Renfro Valley Motel in Renfro Valley, Kentucky. The leaves were showing off their new colors, and the hills were vivid. This was the second night of the Smoky Mountains tour. The plan was to get everyone settled, have a boardin' house dinner at the historic Lodge Restaurant, and then enjoy the evening country music show. Simple—right? Not for Don! After eating dinner, people were returning to their rooms to freshen up before going to the jamboree. Don was no exception. When he got to his room, he noticed his wife, Anna, was in the bathroom. The television was on, so he sat on the end of the bed and began clicking through the channels. When Anna came out of the bathroom, he looked up, and it wasn't Anna. In fact, it wasn't even his room! At a loss for words, he didn't utter a sound but got up and quickly left. That was a good icebreaker. The story traveled throughout the coach, and the group had a good laugh.

Same tour, same man, different hotel. The Hampton Inn features very nice breakfasts. They serve a variety of cereals, waffles, breads, juices, and boiled eggs. The breakfast room was full, and people were eating or preparing their food. I was at the desk close by, taking care of the bill. It was noisy, with people talking and laughing. A loud explosion filled the room. Chairs scraped; someone screamed. Turning around, I expected to see people ducked under tables; but what I saw was Don with his eyes big and his mouth open. He had blown up a boiled egg in the microwave. The microwave door was blown open. His egg and the Styrofoam cup he had had it in were all over the room. Not one piece was bigger than the fingernail on your pinkie finger. Just so you know, Anna is resigned; she smiles and shakes her head.

This same couple signed up for the Texas tour. Our group had visited the oldest mission in San Antonio, the Alamo. This is where 188 brave men volunteered to die defending the Alamo against 2,400 Mexicans. Among the men who died were Davy Crockett, Jim Bowie, and William Travis. The group was walking back to the bus, which was parked about a block away, at the side of the Davy Crockett Hotel. Anna and I were walking together, visiting and talking about who knows what, maybe the events that took place there. Don was walking ahead of us, and he turned around to join in the conversation, walking backward, not looking where he was going. All of a sudden, he turned around again and smacked into a parking sign; everyone around burst out laughing.

Same man, Don. We were on a tour returning across Lake Michigan on the USS *Badger*, a car ferry. Arriving in Manitowoc, Wisconsin, we went to lunch. Don told me that he had left his fanny pack with his camera in it behind the door in the bathroom on the ferry. By that time, the group was eating and the *Badger* was reloaded and had left the dock. I told him I'd call the office and have them contact the boat to check if his camera had been found. Next, we went to the Maritime Museum. He left his jacket behind the door on a hook in that bathroom. I don't remember if we got the camera back, but I think we rescued his jacket. Don has earned a reputation, and when he is on board, we all wonder what will happen to Don.

Chapter 2

The Appalachian mountain range stretches along the eastern shore of the United States. Within this range are smaller mountain ranges. In Vermont, they are called the Green Mountains. We visited these on the New England tour. This tour goes at the end of September and continues into October, when the leaves are at their peak. Remember the gold-, green-, and orange-swirled carpets of the seventies? When you look at the low-lying mountains, the colorful trees remind you of these carpets. You find yourself repeating over and over again, "Isn't this beautiful?"

Our fifth night was spent in the pretty New England town of Stowe, Vermont, nestled in the Green Mountains. Our coach pulled into a little resort on the edge of town. After all of the participants went to their rooms, I began cleaning the coach: emptying the garbage bags, returning the seats to their upright positions, and putting up the footrests. One of the men on the tour returned to the coach and told me his wife wouldn't stay in their room because she had seen a mouse. I was hurrying because we had dinner reservations at 6:00 PM and I wanted to get the bus done before dinner. I told him I'd trade rooms with him. We both walked to his room to move his bags into my room. I was surprised to see the suitcases sitting wide open with no one around. The mouse could have jumped into the suitcases. (I was secretly hoping it did.) He closed the bags, and we carried them to my room. I grabbed my clothes and put them in their room. I didn't stay any longer than to wash my hands. I came out of the bathroom and was going to retrieve my purse, which I had put on the bed. I saw the mouse crawling up the strap and heading into my purse. I said, "Oh, no you don't!" and grabbed a towel and threw it over my purse; then I carried the purse outside and set it on the ground. When I took the towel off, the mouse jumped down and ran away. It didn't really look like a mouse; I think it was a mole looking for a warm place to spend the winter. Later, when I talked to my coworkers at Rustad's, I told them the story. When I got back, I had a package of mousetraps sitting on my desk.

Another story about Stowe! This story actually starts in the Adirondack Mountains. We stopped at McDonald's in Lake Placid, New York, to get a sandwich or a bowl of soup. When we came out of the restaurant, there was a big puddle of fluid under the motor of the coach. We couldn't leave or start the coach until it was fixed. Horrors! What do you do? The driver, Mike, called Rustad's. They located a mechanic that would come to look at it and see if they could fix it well enough to get us to Stowe. But what were we to do while it was getting fixed? It's hard to keep thirty-eight people occupied in McDonald's parking lot. As luck would have it, one of Lake Placid's school bus drivers was in the restaurant, and he gave me the phone number for the school bus company. I called, and they sent a school bus to pick us up and take us to the Olympic site, where the Winter Olympics were held in 1932 and 1988. We spent an hour there watching the ice skaters and looking in the gift shop. We waited another fifteen minutes in the parking lot before Mike came with the coach, repaired well enough to send us on our way. We were an hour late for the Lake Champlain ferry, but they saved a spot for us on a later ferry. We were late getting to Stowe, Vermont, for our dinner, but all were very nice about the delay.

The next morning, we had a part coming for the bus, so we hung around and got to do some things we wouldn't have been able to do otherwise. We visited Emily's Bridge. It is said a ghost named Emily haunts the historic covered bridge, and people refuse to cross it after dark. She is not just a spooky presence that gives people a fleeting glimpse before disappearing into nothing. She gets violent, shaking cars, scratching, and slashing victims with unseen claws.

We also visited the von Trapp family lodge. When Georg von Trapp and Maria left Austria with the children and saw the mountains of Stowe, they knew they had found their new home. Out of their story came the musical *The Sound of Music.* While the mechanic put the new part in the motor of the coach, Rustad's provided funds for the group to eat lunch downtown wherever they chose.

Chapter 3

Speaking of bus breakdowns, there haven't been many, but one breakdown comes to mind whenever the subject comes up. We were on our way to Alaska on a twenty-five-day tour. We were thirty-five miles from Saskatoon when the driver, Chuck, pulled the coach onto the shoulder of Highway 16 and simply stated that we might have a problem. He opened the door and went down the steps to the rear of the motor coach to check the motor. It didn't seem possible that anything could be wrong; he had just had a new motor installed so we wouldn't have any trouble. Returning, he said, "It's not good! The bus company is for sale. Do I have any buyers?" Whatever had happened made it impossible for us to move. I followed him out, and we went to the back of the coach. We were looking at the motor when this big, black car pulled up behind us. The man driving was also dressed all in black. He and Chuck peered into the back of the coach, and as luck would have it, he had all the telephone numbers we needed to get another motor coach out to pick up the people and the telephone number for a wrecker to move our coach to a garage, plus he had the number for a reputable repair shop. It is said every person has an angel watching over them; I swear this was Chuck's angel. This guy didn't leave until he was sure a wrecker and motor coach were on the way. The people began gathering up their belongings, as we didn't think they should leave anything on the coach. We didn't know for sure if we'd see it again. Chuck began unloading luggage and setting it along the side of the highway. People got off and were standing in the ditch. Some stood by the luggage and had their pictures taken hitchhiking. What a spectacle we must have been. There are always treats under the coach. We got out the Cracker Jacks for a late afternoon snack, and then the mosquitoes snacked on us!

The wrecker arrived first and began disconnecting the back wheels. A motor coach can't be towed unless the transmission is disengaged. Soon, it was being hooked up to the wrecker. Thankfully, the other motor coach arrived, so we weren't left standing around in the ditch. Luggage was loaded, and everyone was seated; then we continued on to North Battleford, where we spent the night. We called the hotel and told them we would be late and asked if they would make a soup-and-sandwich supper for the group, compliments of Rustad Tours. It was 8:00 PM before we got to the hotel and were able to eat. That is late for Minnesota people, who are on a 6:00 PM supper schedule.

Chuck's young son, eight-year-old Thomas, was with us on this tour. It would have been fine if he had wanted to stay with the group, but he wanted to be with his dad. Chuck and Thomas went with the wrecker. At night, they stayed with the tow truck driver's mother. During the day, they shopped and hung around the garage. In my book, the Canadians are nice, hospitable people.

We had a new motor coach and a new driver the next morning. The driver's name was Jim. He was very professional and very kind, and everyone really liked him. He had never been to Alaska before and was excited about going. He took me to the grocery store to buy picnic supplies for a group picnic we had planned at Liard Hot Springs. When we arrived there, he helped set up the picnic while I walked the group down to the springs. Walking along the boardwalk, we saw animal tracks of both moose and bear, but thankfully didn't see the animals themselves. Some of the people brought their suits and sat in the mineral water; some rolled up their pants and waded. When they returned to the picnic area, lunch was ready.

I just would like to add a postscript. It was lucky that we didn't see any animals at Liard Springs when we stopped there for a picnic lunch. On a later tour, we made the same stop, and a few days after we had been there, a woman and her son were killed by a bear. Neither a ranger nor her other son could save them.

Jim was with us for three days but didn't get to Alaska. The coach was repaired, and Chuck drove day and night to catch up with us. Thomas sat in the front seat to keep Chuck company and made tuna fish sandwiches for them to eat; they slept in the coach when they got tired. It was two AM when the phone rang and it was Chuck. He was in the parking lot of the

Watson Lake Motel in Watson Lake, Yukon. They slept in the coach that night. I went out and woke them in the morning. Chuck and Thomas used my room to clean up while I cleaned the inside of the coach. Jim was very disappointed that he didn't get to go on, but he helped load the luggage and returned to Saskatoon, Saskatchewan. We went on to Alaska.

Like all drivers, Jim gets around. He had a group to take to Minneapolis, and after dropping the group, he drove over two hours to the office in Kerkhoven just to say hi. Neither Chuck nor I were around. Some of the drivers have met him on the road, and he always approached them to visit. I saw him once after that, on another twenty-five-day Alaska tour. He happened to be driving by the hotel in North Battleford and saw our coach. He stopped at the hotel and asked who the tour director was. The girl behind the hotel desk wouldn't tell him. He said if he could tell them my name, would they call me, and they did. I called Chuck, and both of us went down and had coffee with him. The next morning, he returned to join me for breakfast; he brought everyone in the group a lapel pin. That was very nice.

Chapter 4

Poor Mike! He was my primary driver for many years. If I was going to do something embarrassing or stupid, he usually bore the brunt of it. This incident happened on one of our Alaska tours. We were tooling up the Alaska Highway. Everyone was enjoying the scenery, visiting, and looking for animals. The music was playing softly in the background. I saw a mosquito land on Mike's bald head. Without even thinking, I picked up my itinerary (which was quite thick), held it securely in both my hands, and *whack!* I killed the mosquito. Mike just sank into his seat. I apologized all over the place; honestly, I hadn't even thought anything about Mike. I giggle even as I tell you this, as the look on his face was priceless. We laugh about it now, and when he tells the story, he can embellish it even more.

He can also get into trouble all by himself. We were in Prince Rupert and needed to be up very early to board the Alaska Marine Highway Ferry. It was about 9:00 PM; I had just washed my hair and gotten out of the tub when the phone rang. It was Mike. He said he thought he had broken his arm. I asked how he had done that.

He said he had slipped when he got out of the tub and skidded across the bathroom floor, hitting the toilet stool before slamming into the wall under the sink. I was horrified. I said he had to go to the hospital to check it out, but did I need to go along? I always go with the people when they go to the hospital (but I was wet, and my hair was a mess). He said he could go alone and got a shuttle from the front desk. I forgot to tell him to call when he was back, and I waited and waited. Finally, about midnight, I called the desk, and they had brought him back around 11:30 PM. Then it was necessary to wait until morning to see what damage had been done. When he came down, his arm was in a sling and strapped to his body. His rotor cup was torn, and he needed surgery. (Thanks, Mike, for waiting for that till you got home.) The baggage boys helped him load the luggage; he drove the motor coach with his left arm and the limited use of his right one. I don't know how he did it, but he drove onto the ferry and got it parked. I didn't laugh until he told me he had looked like a walrus sliding across the floor and under the sink. Now I picture that and laugh like crazy. The tour went on with Mike driving. The men on the tour helped with the suitcases, and we worked together keeping the coach clean. It's all well that ends well.

This event happened on our Yellowstone tour. Some of the group needed a ride uptown to find a restaurant. After dropping them off, Mike and I went for fuel, cleaned the bus, and then picked the group up to return them to the hotel. Then it was our turn to go eat. We sat across from each other in a booth, and both of us ordered nice meals; we were hungry. Talking and eating shouldn't be a problem. (Do you think?) Mike burst out laughing, and I looked up and almost died. My sweet corn was running down Mike's glasses. Now he has a grand time telling people, "If Alice is eating sweet corn on the cob, do not sit across the table from her—it's dangerous."

One time, I led Mike astray. We had checked into the Best Western at Nags Head, North Carolina. After finishing our work, we walked to a restaurant about a block away. It was extremely busy that night, and we assumed there would be a waiting list, since people were lined up by the door. I asked the girl in front of us if this was the line for the dining room. She said, "Yes, just put your business card in the basket on the table." I thought that was odd, but I dug out a business card, walked over, and dropped it in the basket. The line moved fast. The girl in front of us was very helpful. We must have looked confused, as she told us just to grab plates and help ourselves. So we did. It dawned on both Mike and me that we maybe shouldn't be here, as it seemed to be a private function. It was too late then, so we just smiled and filled our plates. The only tables available were in the bar, so we sat down. We were offered beverages, so Mike had a beer, and I had wine. When we finished eating, we asked where to pay for our meal and then found out it was free; the function was put on by the Convention and Visitors' Center for their invited guests. I'll tell you, Mike and I almost ran out the door. Mike didn't say anything for a while; then he stated, "That is the last time I'm following you anywhere!" We laughed then, and in the morning, we told the group on the bus; they got a good laugh out of the story.

This might be the place to tell you another story; it has nothing to do with Mike. It took place on the Washington, DC tour. We were on a city tour with a local guide, and we stopped for lunch at a deli/Chinese buffet. I waited until the people had their food and were seated before I get my meal. The driver, Gary, couldn't park there, so he just dropped us off and left. I got him a sandwich too (which he hated). Anyway, I got my food and sat with the guide. While we were eating, a piece of my potato salad dropped off my fork and landed on the shoe of a man sitting at the next table. I was going to ignore it but saw the man look down at his shoe. I started to giggle, told him I was sorry, took my napkin, picked up the potato, and wiped the dressing off his shoe. Then he started to laugh too. We began talking; the guide glared at me and then got up and left. I found out he worked for the Library of Congress. I didn't know it, but the Library of Congress is many buildings, not just one. The guide came back and just seemed mad. She said we had to go; I told her I was still eating. I looked around, and some of the group were still at their tables. She said, "We have to go." I said goodbye to the man, threw my food in the garbage, went out on the sidewalk, and stood by her. Then she asked if I had called the driver. I said, "No."

The guide said, "Call him!" So I did. It took about five minutes for him to come get us. I could have finished eating. She was sure upset about something. Maybe she didn't want me talking to this man, or maybe she just thought I was a pig.

Before we went into the restaurant for lunch, I had put the video camera behind the driver's seat. When Gary got up to go help the people out of the bus, the camera slid under the seat. Gary got in and sat down, smashing the camera under a steel bar. I had a hard time getting the camera out, and when I did, just saying it was broken is putting it mildly. It was destroyed! That evening, I asked at the desk where there was a store where I could get a new camera. The guy behind the desk told me it was easiest to cross the street to the Metro and take the train to Pentagon City. The train stops inside the mall, and we could find camera shops there. Did he know who he was talking to? I toyed with the idea of just going alone, except it was getting dark. I called Gary and asked if he wanted to go for a subway ride. He said, *"What?"* When I told him why, he agreed to go along with me, and I'm really glad he did. The Metro is way below the ground; we went down, down, down before we even got to the trains. Then we needed to get tickets. Let me tell you here that the people of Washington, DC, are very nice when they see a couple of country people trying to figure out the city transportation system. The train traveled under the Potomac River to Pentagon City, where we got off the train. When the man at the desk told me we would get off at the mall, I thought we'd get off in the mall. There was no mall around. Following the crowd, we went up, up, up and did eventually come to the stores. We checked the mall map and found Radio Shack. Gary seemed to know a lot about cameras and picked out a good one. Then it was down, down, down, buy another ticket, take a train ride, and then go up, up, up, ending up across the street from our hotel. I'll tell you one thing: if it weren't for Gary, I'd still be wandering around underground in Washington, DC.

Chapter 5

Medicine Hat is a city in Alberta, Canada, along Trans-Canada Highway 1. The tours go through the city about three times a year. Sometimes we stay overnight, and sometimes we just stop for a coffee break. My first and last experience with a waterslide was at the Medicine Hat Lodge. The slide began on the fourth floor and ended in a five-foot pool of water. I don't like water, I don't like getting my face wet, and I can't swim. How I was ever talked into trying it, *I don't know!* The driver who was my boss, Chuck, and I rode the elevator to the fourth floor. Chuck got on the slide and zoomed down first. I got on the slide, hung onto the sides with both hands, spread my legs really wide, and went down the waterslide really slowly. A little girl came zipping down behind me. One of her legs went around my waist on the right side, and her other leg wrapped around my waist on the left; we continued down the slide really slowly. At the bottom, we slid into the pool slowly and easily, not getting my face wet. I had to laugh and told her she'd better go up and try it again. I promised her I'd stay off the slide.

Attached to the Medicine Hat Lodge is a casino. On one of our overnight stays, two couples on tour went to the casino. One man won big! I didn't find out how much, but his friend told me they wouldn't give him the check, but were mailing it to his home address. It was enough money to pay for the seventeen-day tour for both him and his wife. Sometimes we arrive in Medicine Hat for a coffee stop at McDonald's, located next door to the Medicine Hat Lodge. While the group was having coffee, a mother and adult daughter ran next door to the casino. When they returned less than thirty minutes later, they had won thirty-five dollars. I'm not condoning gambling, as I know they are not in the business to lose money; I'm just telling you of their good luck.

Sometimes for rest breaks we use rest areas along the roadways and interstate highways. You can't travel the country without experiencing outdoor biffys. We stopped at one by Brooks, Alberta. It was a windy day but not cold. There were outhouses for restrooms; they were clean and had toilet paper, so it wasn't bad. The driver and I set up drinks and snacks for the group. We noticed the women coming out of the toilet laughing. Only when they explained that the outhouses didn't go all the way to the ground and the wind was blowing up the holes did I realize that maybe we should have stopped sooner or gone down the road farther.

Another outhouse story concerns my boss, Chuck, and it happened to him before I began working for the company. It makes me laugh, and I do tell his story (once in a while) on the coach. While traveling over the

Canadian Rockies in British Columbia, they stopped to use outhouses and set up lunch at a picnic site. One of the men came out of the restroom and told Chuck he had dropped his glasses down the hole. Now, Chuck is very accommodating; he went under the coach to find a clothes hanger, bent it into a long hook, and was heading to the outhouse. The man began to laugh and then pulled his glasses out of his pocket. He had just wanted to know what Chuck would do. Chuck must have been happy that he was stopped before he began digging in the muck, yuck!

I only know one other restroom story, and maybe I shouldn't tell it, as it could be too embarrassing. But I will, and I'll try to keep it clean. This one took place along the Alaska Highway, where there just aren't too many choices as to where to stop. This outhouse was one double building. A door on one side opened to the ladies' quarters, and a door on the other side opened to the men's. The driver and I wondered about all the noise and laughter coming from the building. It turned out to have two holes on each side, and from the seat down, it was wide open; the only wall was from the ceiling to the seat. So you weren't just going with a friend—you were going with the people on the other side. It seemed that one lady had dressed in the dark that morning and had gotten a pad on upside-down. The men on the other side didn't just chuckle; they came out doubled over in laughter. I still wonder about what exactly went on (and what was said) on the ladies' side.

Chapter 6

Speaking of outhouses, I can add a couple of crappy tales. If you're eating and reading, I suggest you put this down until you've finished eating. Both stories took place in Alaska, probably because there are no McDonald's or Burger Kings every few miles. In fact, towns and small villages can be a hundred miles apart. You may see a small lodge of sorts along the road, but many of those have been closed and are in different stages of disrepair. After traveling all day, we checked into our motel in Fairbanks. The people were settled, and I was cleaning the coach. The driver was washing windows. I opened the restroom door and checked the toilet and then wished I hadn't. The water in the toilet had leaked out, and someone had taken a big dump. (I'm putting that delicately.) Toilet paper had glued itself to the mass, which was partially dried. I went and got the driver to show him. He went to his room, got a wastepaper basket, lined it with a garbage bag, found a clothes hanger, formed that into a hook, and returned to present it to me; then he left. (I don't blame him and hold no grudges.) I dug and dipped and hauled for a good thirty minutes before we could add water, swish, drain, and spray. But it was clean, and in the morning, the coach smelled pretty darn good again.

As I've said, there aren't a whole lot of places to stop along Alaska's roadways; in fact, places to even pull over are few and far between. Except when we see animals, if no one is coming, we just stop and look. It was after lunch, and we were traveling on a long stretch of road in the middle of nowhere in the Yukon. Our destination was Destruction Bay, population fifty-five. Word came up from the back that someone was sick in the toilet. I walked back there and could smell the problem. At that time, I had no clue who was sick or what exactly had happened. I asked through the door if everything was okay. The answer came back, *"No!"* She said she needed her suitcase, as she had to change clothes. I told her to hang on and we'd find a place to pull over to get what she needed. The place we found a few miles further on was a large pull-off with garbage barrels and nothing else. The driver stopped, and all of the group members got off the coach to stretch their legs and walk in the woods. Her husband helped Mike find her bag. Mike also got her a pail of water to wash herself. After she had cleaned up, we put her clothes in a garbage bag and stored them under the coach. I got a clean pail of water and went to wash the toilet. It looked like someone had exploded in there! Stuff was all over: on the floor, on the door, and covering the seat. Good thing there were vinyl gloves on the coach. I scrubbed and then sprayed. The group re-boarded, and we were on our way. Checking into the motel in Destruction Bay, I spotted a guest laundry room. I found the couple and told them where she could wash her clothes and handed her the bag. She remarked that she didn't want the clothes and walked over to a garbage can and threw them away. If I were her, I probably wouldn't have wanted them either. I sympathize with her embarrassment.

When we first began traveling the Alaska Highway, we stayed in cute little cabins. They were very simple, a bed and bathroom. Stopping there worked well for a couple of years until the plumbing went haywire. Someone flushed the toilet in one cabin, and everything came up in the bathtub next door. Back to the drawing board; the tour was revised. Now when you drive by these cabins, everything is boarded up tight.

A couple other incidents that happened in Fairbanks (that I could tell you about) have nothing to do with crappy tales, but one is a pretty hot item. After finishing up one evening upon arriving in Fairbanks, I went for a walk around the block. I was surprised to see a well-dressed man climbing out of a boarded-up fast food stand. The building was small, about the size of a ten-foot-square room. It was the type of place where you order at a window and take your food with you. I arrived at the same time that a man in a suit, white shirt, and tie was climbing out through a large opening in a boarded-up door. Ten or fifteen minutes later, we heard a fire truck, I walked to the corner and looked; it was that same building that was on fire. I didn't know what to do—if I should report what I saw or forget about it. I haven't forgotten about it, but I didn't report it either.

Another time at the same motel, we were cleaning the coach and washing windows; we saw a man digging food out of the dumpster and putting it in a bag. We always have leftover goodies underneath in the bay from our rest stops, so Chuck gathered them together and offered them to the man. He was very grateful and said, "I thank you, my wife thanks you, and my kids thank you." We thought he'd quit digging in the dumpster and go home, but he didn't. When we left, he was still digging for food.

Probably the oddest thing we ever saw on the Alaska tours happened in Tok. It was in the evening at the hotel. I was inside the coach cleaning, and Chuck was outside scrubbing. He got my attention and pointed to the parking lot next door. Lo and behold, there was a semi truck parked, an elephant was standing on a platform outside the trailer, and the driver was giving him a bath. He and Chuck were using the same type of brush. The only difference was that the elephant turned himself around so his other side could be scrubbed. Chuck had to turn the bus around himself so he could scrub the other side.

Chapter 7

Sometimes we have given rides to people in distress. Mostly, it has involved women and children; it seemed like the right thing to do. The first time it happened was a cold, rainy morning in Beaver Creek, Yukon. There were motorcycles at the lodge by milepost 1202 of the Alaska Highway. It was a group of young couples riding to Alaska. One of the cycles had broken down. They had found someone to haul it to Tok to be fixed, but had no way to get there themselves. Chuck (who owned the coach) was driving the tour; he called the office to see if it would be okay for them to ride with us for a couple hours. It was, so that man and lady had a warm ride to Tok while their friends braved the rain and cold.

The second time it happened was along the Ice Field Parkway in Banff National Park, Alberta. The manager of the Crossing, a resort where we had spent the night, asked us if we could give a family a lift to Lake Louise. Their car had died and had been towed there for repairs; it was now ready. Mike and I didn't know what to do because of insurance and liability. So we called the office and asked if it would be all right to be Good Samaritans. We were given the go-ahead. The family consisted of a man, a woman, and two children. They were from Quebec. The woman spoke a little English and the man none. I don't know if the children did or not; they probably knew some from school. We stopped for a couple of picture stops along the way to Lake Louise and then dropped them off at the repair shop. Everything went well. It is not something to make a practice of because things can happen. They could have been a twentieth-century Bonnie and Clyde plotting to rob everyone.

The last time we were asked to help someone was on Johnson Ridge at the top of Mount St. Helens. Two young couples and their children had been camping at the foot of the mountain and had driven up to the top for the day. They had shut their car off in the parking lot, and when they were ready to leave, it wouldn't start. They had been working with it awhile already and did have a tow truck coming to the rescue. The young dad who approached us just asked us to take their wives and children back down the mountain and drop them off by the campground. They felt they could trust a bus full of senior citizens with their families. The men were staying with the car. After the women and kids got off the coach at the campsite, we continued to Seattle. Every evening, when I cleaned the coach, I saw this black jacket lying on the card table. I figured it belonged to someone in the group and they would pick it up when they got cold. The last day of the tour, I went back and picked up the jacket and asked whom it belonged to. No one claimed it. I said, "This is too nice of a jacket to not claim. It has to belong to someone."

Still no one claimed the jacket. Someone suggested it must belong to one of the women who rode down the mountain. Then I felt bad that she had forgotten it; we never got her name, so it couldn't be returned. She could have gotten the 800 number off the back of the coach if she had discovered it fast enough. The end of the story is that I got a very nice jacket. I've worn it for years, and it's looking a little tatty, but it's still serviceable and is the first jacket I grab out of the closet.

Chapter 8

I know I've used a lot of paper telling you stories about Alaska, and I have just a few more. It's not that I don't go anywhere else, but the most interesting episodes are apt to happen on longer tours and in remote areas. Our group left Whitehorse, Yukon, and was traveling south on Highway 2 to Skagway. We met a gravel truck, and when he passed, a good-sized rock fell off and hit the driver's window in the lower right-hand corner. The rock made a small hole with a spiderweb of shattered glass around it. Glass shards flew back to the second seat on the coach. People ended up with glass on their laps, and I was picking glass shards out of my arm. It is illegal to drive with a broken driver's window. There was also nothing we could do about it until we got home.

In the past, we've stopped in the town of Glennallen, Alaska, to spend the night before traveling to Valdez. On this one occasion, we were going to have a morning picnic. We ordered some scrumptious homemade rolls from their kitchen and thirty cups of coffee. After filling the thirty-cup coffee pot, I set it on the card table in the rear of the coach. I have no clue to as what

I was thinking (or maybe not thinking at all). It could have been an unconscious test of the driver's skills. The driver left the parking lot, stopped at the corner, and turned left; then, *bang!* The coffee pot hit the floor, and thirty cups of coffee came pouring down the aisle. The driver stopped and got the mop and pail out from underneath the coach. I mopped and wrung, mopped and wrung, and got as much as humanly possible mopped up with thirty-eight pairs of shoes in the way. We learn from our mistakes, don't we?

A few years later, we again stayed overnight in Glennallen, and I almost got kicked out of the motel. The evening was uneventful, and there was no hint as to what was to come. I ironed my clothes and went to bed about nine o'clock. At midnight, I was sound asleep when the TV set came on as loud as possible (behind my head) in the next room, accompanied by loud talking and laughter. I sat straight up in bed, madder than a wet hen. I banged on the wall and yelled, *"Turn that TV down!"* It immediately went down. I lay back down and pulled the covers up, and my phone rang. It was the desk attendant, and he was mad. He told me if I didn't quiet down in my room, I'd be asked to leave. *Go figure!* I didn't make any more noise, as I didn't want to go sleep in the bus.

We've done our share of good deeds over the years. It is always nice to help people if you can. The Top of The World Highway is a dirt road known as Highway 9 in Canada and Highway 5 in Alaska. It goes from Dawson in the Yukon to end at the Alaska Highway, between Tetlin Junction and Tok. From Dawson, you drive onto a small ferry that brings you across the Yukon River, and then the road winds up out of the valley. Before you reach the border, standing stately on the horizon are two primitive outhouses. It is a good place to stop, as the view is breathtaking even though you hold your breath as long as possible. At the border, they stamp your passport "Poker Creek, Alaska." Between there and the Alaska Highway, there is one place to stop, in the small town of Chicken, population twenty-five nice people and one old grump. Along the road, there is a little store that sells some groceries and souvenirs. An outhouse is the only facility available.

While we were here, a pickup truck pulled up with three young men. One of the boys was quite agitated. He needed a pay phone, as his cell phone wasn't working. There was no pay phone in town. I asked him what was wrong. He said he lived at the North Pole, they were camping for the weekend, and he had left without asking his neighbor to watch his dog. The dog was locked in the garage, and he was afraid he wouldn't be fed or watered all the while he was gone. I asked for the name of the person and telephone number and said I would call her when I got to the North Pole. He seemed really relieved. When we reached the Santa Claus House at the North Pole, I called the number and relayed the message. The lady said she'd go over right away and see to the dog. Everything is well that ends well.

God winks happen too! When something nice happens, we say that God winks at us and shows us something wonderful. The same year I took my grandson, Chad, with us to Alaska to help with the luggage is when we saw the biggest brown bear you can imagine. We were coming up the mountain out of Skagway when off to the right side of the coach, this huge beast was walking along the edge of the forest. With every step he took, his shiny coat rippled in the sunlight. It was the most awesome thing. Mike stopped in the road, and all of the tour members were clicking their cameras. We all got some of the most impressive photos before he disappeared into the forest. There are usually some animals around for us to admire, but none like this trophy bear.

The Lower Forty-eight also has its overwhelming animal sightings. Leaving Sheridan, Wyoming, and traveling west over the Bighorn Mountains, we saw a large bull moose walking down a hill toward the road. We watched in awe as he picked one foot up after the other and effortlessly stepped over the fence and then sauntered toward a creek for a drink of water. It's not unusual to see animals in the Bighorns, but usually it's cattle, and sometimes they are on the road being herded by cowboys.

Yellowstone National Park is a great place for animal encounters. Many times, we find ourselves behind a buffalo or two that won't yield to traffic. So we putt-putt-putt behind until they get good and ready to move off the road. Except (there is always an exception to the rule) when a whole herd of buffalo decide to cross the road in front of the traffic. We waited patiently for them all to cross over; then the leaders of the herd decided the other side of the road was better, and they all crossed over again. Don't tell me they don't know what they are doing! They crisscrossed the road a few more times until the cars began to slowly push through. Then they scattered to the ditches on either side of the road. We reached the fishing bridge general store; the driver (a different Mike) unloaded us at the door and left to park. That was when the herd of buffalo caught up and surrounded the coach. Poor Mike couldn't even get out. He couldn't have gotten the door open if he had dared to. The buffalo didn't leave until it was time to pull up and pick us up again.

Chapter 9

Besides traveling in the United States and Canada, we've done some overseas tours traveling with other companies, such as Globus and Collette. We've always had excellent guides and good experiences. Unusual things happen on their tours too! On the Continental Introduction, you visit England, France, Switzerland, Italy, Germany, and Holland. It is a very fast-paced tour, and a person needs to be in pretty good shape and willing to roll with the punches. My sister Gin came with on this tour. It was very nice to have someone to hang with and to help. Out of our twenty-eight tour members, we had four older people; this particular tour was very hard for them. Let's call the three ladies Sophie, Marcella, and Verna. The man we'll call Norm. We also had one grumpy old man; let's name him Alfred. He complained about everything: his bed, the ferry, food, waitress, service, and his poor wife. In fact, one hotel restaurant called the company and reported that he had sworn at the waitress. The tour director told me if he didn't shape up, they would ask him to leave the tour. The hotel told their company they couldn't use their property anymore. Our local guide, Jeanne, had to write up a report. He must have shaped up, because he came home with the group. Tours aren't for everyone.

In Amsterdam, we visited the diamond factory and then rode the coach past the brothels on the way to the canal for a boat cruise. The people got a chuckle out of the girls who were standing in the windows under the red awnings in their white-and-black bikinis. By the way, did you know that Amsterdam is 5,397 miles from Wall Drug?

Germany is known for beer, mountains, and music. We visited Munich and drove past a castle built by Ludwig I. Ludwig was a womanizer; a pretty woman would catch his eye, and he would have her portrait painted and hung in the palace. He called his palace Nymphenburg. In front of the palace is a little pond with ducks, geese, and swans. Ludwig II was the builder (known as Mad Ludwig). He built three castles and cost the country almost all its money. The castle at Disneyland is said to be patterned after one of his creations. We got off the coach in the city of Munich, and Jeanne walked with us to St. Mary's Square. Outdoor cafés and little shops surrounded the square. A fountain sat in the middle of the square, and that was to be our meeting place. Some of us walked to the beerhouse called Hofbräuhaus. It was a lively place with a band playing oom-pa-pa music, lots of beer, and huge pretzels. It was a fun place that made me wish I liked beer. Back at the fountain in the square, the funniest thing happened. A wino or street person was sitting on the side of the fountain. He took off his shoes and stockings; then he turned around and put his feet in the fountain. Another man came across the square with his whiskey bottle; he filled it with water from the fountain next to the man washing his feet. He walked back across the square drinking the water from the bottle. I guess it is a sad thing, but the people who saw it happen got a kick out of the incident.

In Rome, Italy, after seeing the Coliseum, we went to St. Peter's Square. The Pope was having an audience and was sitting in a chair under an awning. They had delivered him to the square in an old pickup truck. The crowd was so thick you couldn't get close for a picture. I did take one with the video camera and zoomed in to bring him as close as possible. (It was a shaky picture!) Gin and I walked to the meeting place to wait for our guide, Jeanne, who was taking us on a tour of the cathedral. The lady who was sharing a room with Verna came to me and said that she had shown the three older ladies where the restrooms were and then left them. She said she was tired of taking care of them and hadn't come on the trip to baby-sit. I told her she didn't have to be with Verna all the time if it was ruining her vacation; they were just sharing a room. It was my job to watch out for them. That seemed to satisfy her, and she went off. Gin and I got a cup of coffee and sat down on a cement ledge with Sophie and Marcella. Sophie said to me, "We haven't seen Verna for a long time." I asked where she had last been seen, which was just across the street in the restaurant toilet. It didn't seem possible for her to get lost going across the street, but I began searching the crowd of people, hoping to see her coming. I didn't think she could not be there, as we hadn't moved from that area. I turned and saw her sitting on a cement bench, flushed and shaky, trying to open a can of Coke. I walked over to her, took her pop, and opened it. Handing it back to her, I asked what had happened. When she had come out of the toilet in the restaurant, Sophie and Marcella had left her. She went outside, and everything looked strange. She turned and walked away from us rather than just coming across the street. She became lost, walking farther and farther away. The farther she walked, the more agitated she became. She missed her step and fell off the curb into the street of busy traffic. She told me everyone came to her, picked her up, and got her back on the sidewalk. She could have been hit by a car, and I wouldn't have known. Somehow, she got turned around and made it back before the guide came to take the group into the Basilica of St. Peter. Her hand was swollen and bruised, her knee was skinned and hurting, and her clothes were dirty. I thought she should see a doctor, but she said no. You can't force them, just offer. Neither Verna nor Norm, who had fallen down three steps the night before, could keep up, so I stayed back with them and let them rest. We then slowly walked to the gathering place to wait for the group. Both of them felt better after sitting in the shade and resting. Back at the hotel, there were two messages for me. One couple's daughter had had surgery and was doing fine. I had to tell Marcella her landlord had died. He had been killed in a car accident.

The next night, in Florence, the hotel had misplaced two pieces of luggage. We found one easily; it was in our room. It belonged to Ted Wong, who was a Chinese member of the group. We teased him about his suitcase being in the Wong room. The other suitcase took a while to find. When I was getting ice for Verna's sprained and swollen wrist, I found it and brought it to the correct room. Jeanne told me she had never had such an old group and had called all the hotels to warn them. I don't know what the hotels would have done differently.

At the Leaning Tower of Pisa, we lost another lady. Kay and Jan were walking back to the coach, and Jan decided to run back to buy a banana. Kay stayed behind to look at some scarves. Everyone was on the coach, and no Kay. Jeannie got off, and I could see her walking back to find her. I got off and walked around the coach so she could see me when she came back. The driver was there, so I got back on the coach, where I could see out over the heads of the crowd. We watched and waited. Jeannie came back; she asked me what I wanted to do. We had to be going. I told her I didn't want to leave her, but I couldn't stay there either. The two Chinese men got off to go look for her, Jeannie got off again. She talked to another tour director, and he agreed to take Kay along with him when she returned and to help her get a train to the hotel. Everyone came back. She wasn't anywhere; it was like the earth had opened and swallowed her. I envisioned someone hitting her on the head, dragging her into the bushes, and robbing her. Jeannie thought she might have had a stroke or heart attack and had been taken to the medical center. We were going to leave her, as we had been looking and waiting thirty-five minutes already. I looked out the window one more time and saw her coming through the crowd, looking very frightened. We got off to meet her and brought her to the coach. I couldn't even talk to her because I was so upset. These people have got to stick together, if one doesn't remember the instruction, the other might. What a relief to have her back safely.

Traveling back to Paris, we stopped for lunch in a cafeteria. Gin and I got a yogurt and an eight-inch sub sandwich to split. Verna was ahead of us in line. When we got to the end of the line, we noticed she didn't have anything to eat on her tray. I asked her if she had bought something to eat, and she said, "No, I asked for a pork sandwich, and they didn't have any." I divided our sub and gave her a third. (It wasn't a pork sandwich either.)

We got to our hotel in Paris, and more adventures were in store. The hotel had a revolving door that spun very fast. You'd think they could have slowed it down. None of the older people could get through; they stood and looked at the door spinning in front of them. Gin took Marcella and brought her through, I took Sophie and rushed her through, and the grandson traveling with Norm got him through. Then Verna went through by herself and made it, but she stopped and didn't step all the way out. I grabbed her and pulled her forward, but not fast enough; the door hit her in the back. It almost knocked her down. Then at the elevators, the doors were closing so fast the people couldn't get in. Sophie got caught when the door shut on her. I pulled her back, and then I heard an "Oh, shit!" I looked around the corner, and Verna had her sore arm caught in the other elevator door. Gin was trying to open the door with one hand and pull Verna's arm out with the other hand. All of them did finally get to their rooms.

There was a farewell dinner that evening called "Les Noces de Jeannette," which means "The Wedding of Jeannette." The beverages were wine, beer, and Coke. An accordion player strolled throughout the group, playing and encouraging the group to sing. After more wine, everyone was laughing and having a good time. Verna was telling jokes. We all laughed so hard! Walking to that restaurant, we saw a fellow who was slightly inebriated coming down the sidewalk. He must have been very angry. Three local ladies were also walking on the sidewalk; he kicked one of the ladies in the ankle and then went on his way. She was surprised and turned around to look at him. He kicked a building very hard; it must have hurt his toe worse than the wall. Then he looked at our group and my legs. My mind was wondering if he would attack me next. Then he crossed the street and began ripping paper signs off a building.

Later, we did an illumination tour of Paris. We saw the Eiffel Tower and then got off the coach to take pictures. Gin was backing up to get a perfect picture and fell backward over a low fence. I saw her falling and started toward her; I knew I'd never reach her in time to catch her but figured I could pick her up again. Two men were walking by; one caught her and hoisted her up on her feet almost before she hit the ground. It looked so funny everyone roared with laughter. She said she fell for a Frenchman, but they looked more

East Indian to the rest of the group. That night, the driver, the coach, and Jeanne left us on our own. She gave me a gift of French perfume for helping with the group. She said she couldn't have done it alone, and she wouldn't. It was time to go home!

I left 3:30 AM wake-up calls for the group, which didn't go through. I tried to call everyone, but the phones had been shut off. I ended up knocking on everyone's door to make sure all were awake. We didn't have any luggage service for some reason. I had asked for carts the night before, and they had told me I couldn't have any, that they'd be locked up and I could get them in the morning. I told them I wanted them now, as in the morning, there would be someone at the desk who didn't speak English, and I'd never get them. I threatened them too! I told them if I didn't get the carts that night, they had better have someone there at 4:00 AM to pick up our bags. (They gave me two carts, and I put them in our room.) At 4:00 AM, I started picking the luggage up on the seventh floor and then went down to the sixth floor. I met a couple of tour members who were going down to breakfast. The man said I shouldn't be lifting those heavy suitcases, so he stayed to help me. (I was grateful for his help.) This fellow also had a bad heart; the way he was huffing and puffing, I was afraid he'd have a heart attack.

The shuttle bus was late coming to bring us to the airport, and when it arrived, it was a small shuttle without enough room for all the bags to be put underneath in the bay. The driver had very little ambition and wasn't even going to help load the suitcases onto the bus. Since they wouldn't all fit in the bay, we ended up piling the remaining suitcases in the two front seats of the bus and in the aisle. At the airport, we found luggage carts and unloaded the bags and the group; then we began to check in for our flight. It was a slow process. Either the computers were slow, or they had a lot of trainees. I got the group through and came last with my three ladies. Don't you suppose they overbooked and were short a seat for Gin? By the time she found somewhere to sit, we had quite a long walk to get to the plane and not much time. I had just gotten the ladies seated and their bags stowed before the plane took off. That was cutting it close! We needed to change planes in Amsterdam, where there was another really long walk to the next departure gate. It was a good thing we had lots of time, as the girls in Paris had screwed up our seating arrangements. Husbands and wives weren't sitting together, and it was a real hassle. Once everyone was situated on the plane, we had a smooth flight home. Arriving at the Humphrey Airport, we found out one suitcase hadn't arrived. (It was delivered to their home the next day.) Remember the angry, unhappy man, Alfred, who complained about everything and swore at the waitress? His new suitcase was smashed!

This is a good tour. I'd recommend it to anyone who is in good health and able to walk. I'd like to do it again!

Chapter 10

On a Sunday afternoon, our group was returning home from the Pacific Northwest. We were traveling east on Highway 20 in Oregon between the cities of Bend and Burns. It is 130 miles between the towns, with just a smattering of small villages. In fact, I believe there are three, and they are many miles apart. This area is called the High Desert. We were about an hour out of Bend when we met a car. The car was coming toward us and began to veer toward the ditch. It went into the ditch and rolled. Usually, we don't stop for accidents, as there are always people who have already stopped to help and it is upsetting to the group, so we just continue on our way. This time, we had no choice; there were no other vehicles in sight. Chuck was driving and pulled to the side of the road. I got out and ran to the car. The car was lying on its side, and the boy was out of the car, pulling the girl out through the window. She was wearing bib overalls with a tube top; as he pulled her out, he pulled her top right off. The girl was crying and bleeding; he set her on the ground away from the car, where she sank down into the sand. I helped her get dressed and put my arms around her to comfort her. The boy took his fist and hit the car as hard as he could; the car popped right back up onto its wheels. It was the darnedest thing! By that time, Chuck had gotten the bus situated and had joined us. I asked him to go get some water and paper towels and call 911. Then a semi truck stopped, and the driver talked to Chuck. (I guess the trucker called 911.) While Chuck was getting the water to wash the blood off the girl, I learned the story. They were both in high school, and the girl was five months pregnant. The boy had borrowed his brother's car. They had left Wyoming on Saturday night and were on their way to Oregon to be married. Neither of them had slept since Friday night. The girl had fallen asleep in the car; I guess the boy fell asleep at the wheel. The girl kept crying and saying that her dad was going to kill her. I was washing the blood off her face and arms, and I told her that her dad would not kill her. Her parents were probably worried half to death. I made her promise to call them as soon as she got to a phone. Another car stopped, and a man came into the ditch carrying a briefcase. He set it on the ground and opened it. I saw it was full of bandages. He told me that he was a paramedic and asked if he could help. I was happy to put him in charge. The kids seemed to be in good hands: the trucker was still there, an ambulance was on the way, and they had a paramedic. We left! When I got in the bus, I noticed my dress was covered with blood. I got a Wet One and tried to clean it off, but there was too much; it just smeared. I wonder what the desk clerk thought when we arrived at the motel in Burns. I went to the desk to check the group in and pick up the keys covered in blood. I've also wondered many times what happened to those two young people. I hope things worked out well for them.

We have very safe and courteous drivers, and we aren't involved in accidents. But there are always exceptions to the rule. An accident happened on our Nova Scotia and Atlantic province tour. We were in the city of Grand Falls, New Brunswick, on our way to the visitor center to take a break and snap pictures of the falls. If you're not familiar with New Brunswick, it's a Canadian province that shares a border with Maine. Mike was driving the coach through the city on Trans-Canada Highway 2 when a car came out of a McDonald's restaurant on our left, pulled into the left-hand lane, and then turned into our lane right in front of the coach. Mike hit the brakes, but they were right in front of us; he had no room to stop. The car was pushed quite a few feet. Later, we learned the two ladies were from Maine, and they were heading for a road across the highway that said, "Do Not Enter!" The passenger's side of the car was smashed. The woman sitting in the passenger's seat was eating a hamburger with catsup, which smeared all over her face. The ambulance arrived, and they put up a blanket to shield her as she was being removed from the vehicle. I couldn't tell how badly she was hurt. I don't think the driver was hurt. The car wasn't going anywhere; it didn't look drivable. The incident put everyone in a somber mood and held us up for a while. After everything was said and done, it was the ladies' fault completely. How can you not see a bus? They were visiting, eating, driving, and not paying attention.

The coach was hardly scratched, and we were able to continue with the tour.

This next story is really sad. It took place on the third day of our New England tour. We were on our way to Niagara Falls, Ontario. Our group stopped at the Welland Canal in St. Catherine's to watch a ship go through the canal. The Welland Canal was built so ships could travel between the Great Lakes of Lake Erie and Lake Ontario. There was a ship in the lock being lowered to the level of Lake Ontario. The group was out by the ship. Some had gone up the stairs to the catwalk to get a better look. I had been out taking pictures; when I came in, I saw Mike, and he said he had bought me a cup of coffee. We had just sat down at a table when Mike looked up and said, "It looks like someone is down."

I said, "I hope it's not one of our people."

Just as I said that, it came over the intercom: "Will the tour director for Rustad Tours please come to the desk." I got up, ran outside, and ran up the stairs, and it was one of our younger ladies. Some people in our group were up there too. One of the men was holding an umbrella over her to protect her from the light rain that was falling. I knelt by her side. A young Asian girl was cradling her head on her knees.

The injured lady told me she thought she was having a heart attack. She began gagging, so I slipped my arm under her and rolled her to her side so she could throw up; it was yellow gunk that spewed over the catwalk to the sidewalk below. She said, "Aspirin helps with heart attacks. Is there one in my purse?" Her friend looked in her purse, but just found Tylenol. Then she said, "If I don't make it, tell my kids I love them." I told her I would. I'm sure that is when she died. The ambulance had arrived, but the EMTs had trouble getting the gurney up to the catwalk because people were in the elevator. When they made it, she was transported to the ambulance, where they worked on her for fifteen or twenty minutes. They used the paddles, and the ambulance rocked back and forth. They came and told us they were taking her to the hospital and then gave Mike directions so we could follow. I had the group paged to board the coach immediately; then we left for the hospital. When we arrived, Mike dropped her friend and me at the door, where we were met by nurses who ushered us into a room to wait for the doctor. The doctor told us that the biggest vein in her body had burst; she had suffered an aneurism and was gone in six seconds. The chaplain came and talked with us, and then we were allowed to see her. They brought us into a room where we could call her family. It was very hard to call her daughter to tell her what had happened. I did it in the nicest way I knew. I can imagine the shock it must have been to hear the news. The chaplain came back to the coach with us and told the group; he was good at explaining what had happened. The hospital, the chaplain, and the doctors took care of all the arrangements of flying her home. Her friend wanted to go home right away, but I convinced her to stay until we reached Portland, Maine. It would be easier and less expensive to fly home from the United States rather than out of

Canada. In Portland, a taxi picked us up early in the morning, and we rode together to the airport. Once she was on her way, I got another taxi to return to the hotel to meet the group and finish the tour.

Outhouses on the Top of the World Highway - Chapter 5

Border Crossing between the Yukon and Alaska - Chapter 8

Ferry that takes you across the Yukon River - Chapter 8

One of Rustad's deluxe coaches boarding a ferry. – Chapter 1

Storks nesting on the chimneys in Spain - Chapter 13

Eiffel Tower where Gin fell for a Frenchman - Chapter 9

The Red Coat - Chapter 12

Drinking wine at Ayers Rock - Chapter 12

Eating a Witchetty Grub in Australia (not really)
Chapter12

The Columbia space shuttle being launched
February 22, 1996 - Chapter 14

Chapter 11

How do you feel about airplanes? I feel they are the bane of my existence! You have no control over your life when you fly. You're totally at the mercy of circumstances. On one of our Alaska tours, it was proven. That year, there were three Alaska tours. Mike and I drove the group up to Alaska through the Canadian Rockies, across British Columbia on the Yellowhead Highway, and then took the Alaska Marine Highway (ferry) to Skagway. This was a seventeen-day tour. After that tour ended, the group flew home. We met the second group at the airport and toured Alaska. Both Mike and I were to fly home with that group on the eighth day. Another driver, Leon, flew up to drive the third group, which was to arrive the following day with another guide.

We had a 7:30 AM flight and needed to be at the airport two hours ahead of time. We were! The group was all checked in, we had even boarded the plane, and then we sat there. The pilot came on the intercom and announced there would be a fifteen- to twenty-minute delay. He said there was a minor problem with a circuit breaker, and they had to find the problem. At intervals, the pilot would announce that we should be departing soon. At ten-thirty, after we had been sitting on the plane three hours, the pilot said that everyone could leave the plane but could not leave the boarding area. We would be called to re-board in a short time. As we left the plane, everyone was given a voucher for lunch. After eating, we sat around the waiting area listening for news of our flight's departure. At noon, they found the problem. It was a part that ensured that if one motor should quit, the other motor would automatically take over and fly the plane. They said another plane would be arriving at 2:30 PM and they would take that part and put it on our plane. We should be flying by 3:30 PM, they told us. The people talked, slept, read, shopped, and walked. At two thirty, the plane came; they took the part off, and it didn't fit. I asked why they couldn't unload the disabled plane and put our luggage on the other plane and just fly back to Minneapolis on the good plane. I was told it would cost too much to do that. At 4:15 PM, it was announced that our flight was cancelled. The pilots needed to be off-duty for thirteen hours before flying. Angry people just swarmed the counter, all talking at once. The fishermen had fish thawing underneath the plane. A lot of angry words were flying around the terminal.

We were to leave at 7:30 AM the following morning. I had been keeping in touch with Rustad's office, as a coach was meeting us in Minneapolis to take us back to our cars parked at the bus garage. Now we were all still in Anchorage with the coach and driver waiting at the Lindbergh Airport! Okay! A security person asked how many rooms I needed for the group. We needed to find twenty-one rooms so they could get a good night's sleep. The airlines were very nice about helping with that and found us rooms at the Inlet Tower Suites, about ten minutes from the airport. They gave us a voucher to pay for the rooms and a thirteen-dollar voucher per person for dinner. Plus everyone got a voucher for a hundred dollars off on another flight. Wasn't that a lot cheaper than transferring the bags to another plane?

Luggage was not unloaded, so we had no suitcases, just our small bags we carried on the plane. I called the hotel where the driver, Leon, was staying and asked the desk clerk if our coach was parked outside. She said, "Yes!" I asked her to ring the driver's room; there was no answer, so I left a message. I wanted him to come to the airport to get us and take us to the hotel where we were staying. Meanwhile, I called the hotel and had their shuttle come to the airport to transfer the group. The shuttle held about six people, seven if one sat up by the driver. Mike went with the first group so he could start getting people checked into their rooms. I stayed at the airport with the group. Ten minutes for the shuttle get to the hotel, five minutes to unload the people, ten minutes to get back to the airport. It was taking forever! About 5:30 PM, I put the people who were left in a taxi. Arriving at the hotel, I talked to the manager of the restaurant about what they could do to feed the group on a thirteen-dollar-per-person voucher. They put together a very nice salad and pasta buffet bar. One couple had put their insulin in the big suitcase under the plane and couldn't get it back. They took a taxi uptown to the drugstore and then stayed to eat their dinner. That night was the first time I ever slept in a towel; then I lost the towel sometime during the night. Leon picked us up the next morning to shuttle us to the airport. He came early, and we fed everyone Rice Krispie bars and apple juice from the stash under the coach and then returned to the terminal. Our luggage had been transferred to another plane, and the flight home was uneventful. There were a lot of empty seats on the plane. I'm thinking those were the fishermen who flew home with their fish on the red-eye.

Then, why is it that the people who take sleeping pills always have aisle seats? A flight to Australia takes sixteen hours. On the way home from one of the Australia tours, I was stuck in the last row on the plane. I love aisle seats. (I don't take sleeping pills.) I need to use the restroom periodically. There I sat in the last row, the second seat in; the space was so tight I couldn't even bend down to pick up a book out of my bag. The girl on the aisle seat was zonked! After about three hours of sitting, I needed to move, and my bladder was objecting. I couldn't wake her up to get out, so I managed to wiggle around and get my feet on the seat to stand. After I was standing on the seat, I didn't know what to do next. I stepped on my armrest, stepped over the girl, and stood on her armrest; then I wasn't sure how to get down. Thank goodness one of the men in our group was walking down the aisle; he took my arm to help me down. It was such a relief to be standing that I just stood for a long time. To get back to my seat, I climbed back up onto the armrest, stepped over the girl, and then slid into my seat. She didn't wake up for hours. I think she had a balloon for a bladder.

Small planes scare me to death. I didn't know I was afraid of them, as I've been in helicopters, and they aren't scary. We took a group to Australia and New Zealand. After touring some of the South Island, we ended up by the glaciers. The tour director gave the group a choice of flying back to Christchurch or coming back with the coach, which was a two-hour drive. I usually do whatever the majority of my group wants to do, and all but two decided to spend the extra money to fly. At the small airport, they had five small planes waiting. Each one held seven people and the pilot. Since I'm always last, I watched as the planes taxied down the short runway to lift off over the mountains. (Just between you and me, it didn't seem like they would make it.) Then it was our turn. The pilot held the doors open, helped with seat belts, and then secured the door. I was in the third row on the right side by the door. I said to the pilot, "I don't think this is your newest model."

He answered, "No, it is about the same age as the Beatles." I figured they were about forty-five years old at that time. We taxied down the runway; the little plane groaned when it took off and roared as it lifted into the sky. I saw the ocean, and then the pilot banked over the glacier-topped mountains. The plane shook, groaned, and roared. Even through our headsets it was loud. The ladies sitting in front of me never looked up; they sat with their heads bowed the entire trip.

My Aunt Iva was sitting in the front by the pilot; the dashboard was so high she couldn't see over it, so she wasn't frightened. The lady sitting next to me grabbed my left hand and was squeezing it so tightly that my fingers were purple. To keep my cool, I took pictures (one-handed) with the video camera. I pointed it out the window toward the ground. As I looked down between the rugged mountains at patches of green grass, I wondered if any of those patches were large enough to land a plane. I prayed! I promised God if I got back to earth safely, I would never get on another small plane. I won't, either! Maybe in a life-and-death situation, but then it won't matter anyway. The two people who chose to ride back told us it was pretty scary driving back with the coach too! They said the driver was speeding to get the people back in time so they wouldn't be late for the dinner show that evening. He would take the curves around the mountains very fast; they were sliding back and forth in their seats and hanging on for dear life.

Chapter 12

My red leather coat is easy to spot; that's why I wear it in airports. It's starting to look tattered and worn, so Colombo has nothing on me. It can also be used for an extra cover at night when it's chilly. I'll probably be the only ninety-year-old woman walking around in a red leather coat, still trying to get my money's worth. That coat has been with me to Australia and New Zealand three times. The first time was in 1994; that is when I bought a red Aussie hat to go with the red coat. No one ever got lost. The cry was, "Follow the lady in red!"

Getting there is half the fun (or stress). It's a long flight, sixteen hours from Minneapolis, and then in crossing the International Date Line, a day is lost. On this tour, the plane landed in Auckland on the North Island of New Zealand. This island is closer to the equator, so it is more tropical and much warmer. Steam vents spout in the back yards of the Maori people, and they use them for cooking at their backyard barbies. Thermal activities here are similar to those in Yellowstone National Park. One thing that stands out about this island is the glow worms. I didn't even know they actually existed, I thought we just sang about them. You know, "Glow, little glow worm, glitter, glitter." Glow worms are actually the pupa of a fly. The part that glows is waste. The head is at the other end. The glow worm spins a thread and drops it; they can spin and drop forty of these lines. The lines are sticky, and insects get stuck on them. The glow worm then reels the line in, similar to fishing. Then it eats its meal. When the pupa evolves into a fly, it doesn't have a mouth. Its sole purpose is to reproduce. After the female mates and lays her thousands of eggs, she dies. The life span is about four days, and then she starves to death. The cycle starts over again. Our group climbed into small boats and moved slowly into Waitoma Caves. It was awesome! The cave was pitch-black; the glow worms hanging from the ceiling created thousands and thousands of little lights. This was the only time our tour included the North Island. I was sorry the other two groups of tour members didn't get to see this remarkable sight. All the tours have visited the South Island. Here is where the high, towering mountains lie along the western shore. Known as the Southern Alps, they stretch the length of the entire island and are covered with spectacular glaciers. Many visitors come to visit the glaciers in Westland and Mount Cook national parks. Both islands are very different and very beautiful.

Another favorite thing to do in New Zealand is visit the home of a host family for dinner. Families in Queenstown sign up to be host families to four to six people. I have spent an evening with Hallan and Barbara, who were in the insurance business.

Hallan's mother Fay joined us for the meal. When he returned us to the hotel, he gave us a tour of the downtown area where he worked. On my second visit to Queenstown, my host family was Ray and Sandra Drayton. Ray owned a restaurant in Queenstown. He cooked a meal of French crepes, and Sandra made the dessert. Sandra is a teacher, and Ray is an author. He has written four books. I have one of his books; the name of it is *Mother Goose.* It is a World War II story about rescuing children from war zones. Jenny Mason hosted us on the third tour. She had a beautiful house in Queenstown and ran a bed and breakfast from her home. She had overnight guests, who arrived while we were visiting. An interesting thing to note is that all the desserts were Pavlova. This is a light dessert made from meringue topped with whipped cream and fruit. It's delicious. I should learn how to make that yummy dessert.

Australia is a lot like the United States except they are upside down and they talk funny. They say we are upside down and talk funny. Even their toilets flush backward. When we flush our toilets, the water goes down clockwise. When they flush their toilets, the water goes down counterclockwise. This is the only country in the world that I know of where you go out into the outback and line up along a fence, sitting on camp stools, to watch a rock change color. Don't tell me God doesn't have a sense of humor. Imagine him looking down at thirty coaches lined up in the desert and then seeing a thousand people drinking wine, eating cheese and crackers, and watching Ayers Rock. He's got to get a belly laugh out of that scene. Even

I got the giggles when I looked down the line at all those tourists.

I love the outback and the flat desert where the monoliths are the only disturbance. The next day, while exploring them closer, some people climbed to Chicken Point of Ayers Rock in the 106-degree heat. Oh! Did I mention the flies? They were clingy! Flies kissed your cheeks and clung to any other parts of exposed skin. You talked fast so your mouth wasn't open any longer than necessary. We enjoyed a cooking lesson at an evening bush barbie. The bush bread is called "spotted dog." The recipe calls for seven handfuls of flour, seven mouthfuls of water, and salt. You throw in a couple of handfuls of raisins and mix well. Put the dough in a cast-iron kettle with a lid, bury it in the hot coals of the campfire, and let it bake. While it is baking, it is a good idea to move out into the bush away from the light of the fire and look to the heavens. You'd be amazed at the stars in the southern sky. The constellations are very different from what we see in the northern sky. You won't see the North Star or the Big Dipper. Should you decide to wander off into the bush on your own and get lost, don't worry—you won't starve. We learned that you could dig under a witchetty shrub and in the roots you would find the witchetty grub worm. Many people consider this a delicacy. They supply liquid (they're juicy) and food.

Speaking of food, a lady on the tour (let's call her Diane) and I were having lunch at an outdoor plaza in Alice Springs. The plaza was lined with shops and little cafés. Tables were set up outside in the shade of small trees. We both ordered sandwiches from one of the cafés and then took them outside. I ordered a veggie sandwich; Diane had a meat sandwich. I had eaten half of mine and picked up the other half; I was ready to take a bite out of it when this Aborigine man walked up. He held out a handful of change and rubbed his stomach with the other hand. I asked, "Are you hungry? Do you want my sandwich?" He grabbed the other half of my sandwich so fast, put the change back in his pocket, and left. Diane and I looked at each other in astonishment and then burst out laughing. I'll bet he was disappointed when he bit into the lettuce, tomato, and bean sprout sandwich. He could have had Diane's meat sandwich if he had grabbed hers. Anyway, the outback is a favorite place. Where else but Australia can you ride a camel to dinner and eat breakfast with the kangaroos? And flies!

South of Melbourne is Phillip Island Nature Park, the home of the fairy penguins. Penguins are only found in the southern hemisphere. We were told the fairy penguins only exist in two places: on Phillip Island and at the very southern tip of New Zealand. The penguins leave their nests early in the morning and march down to the beach and into the water. They fish all day long! When the sun goes down, you see them coming back to shore. You must be very quiet. If you're not, they get frightened and throw up, and then the babies won't get to eat that day. Baby penguins eat the regurgitated fish. When they come up on the beach, you can tell they are skittish. Some run back to the water and then return. As it gets darker, you can hear the babies calling. The parents answer back. There is a scurry of little penguins marching across the sand and up the dunes, and then they tumble into the holes where their babies are waiting in nests. Some of the parent penguins need to go a long way to reach their nests; they even cross the road to more distant dunes. Early the next morning, they return to the sea for another day of fishing.

If for some unknown reason you end up with a lot of money you should spend and have the choice of buying a new pickup truck or going to Australia, go to Australia and New Zealand. Call me, and I'll go along as your private guide.

Chapter 13

The first commandment of the Traveler's Ten Commandments states that "Thou shalt not expect to find things as thou hast them at home, for thou hast left thy home to find things different."

A small group of ten people, including myself, visited Spain in May of 1997. We flew into Madrid; this was where the group congregated. People flew in from all over to meet and begin their Iberian vacation. For the first couple of days, it didn't look like we were going anywhere, as the bus drivers were on strike in Madrid. While we were waiting around the hotel, a lady from Germany tripped on the step in front of the hotel; she fell into the revolving door, and her head broke the glass. She swore profoundly in German, got up, and walked away. No suing in this country! Our tour director must have had some pull, because he managed to find a coach and driver by ten o'clock the following morning. We left Madrid late to travel to Salamanca. Along the route, we saw huge birds in oversized nests made of sticks and green moss. We were told these were big, white storks that built their nests on roofs, church steeples, towers, and the chimneys of homes. The birds drew a lot of attention as we drove past. In one nest, it looked as if a pair was feeding storklets. The group did the usual sightseeing and made a stop in Segovia to view the aqueduct that was built a couple thousand years ago to bring water to the city from the mountains. The statue of a she-wolf and the twin boys, Romulus and Remus, stood nearby. The twins had been abandoned in the river and were found and raised by the wolf. It is said the twins were the founders of Rome. Salamanca was founded as a Roman settlement in the thirteenth century on the Tarmes River. The Roman bridge crossing the river is two thousand years old. Much of the beautiful architecture dates back hundreds of years.

The scenery from Salamanca to the Portugal border was flat farmland where they raised wheat, potatoes, and sugar beets in their irrigated fields. At the border, the country's sign had twelve stars circling the name *Portugal.* This stood for a united Europe, or the European Union. They were in the process of creating a country with one leader with representatives for each country, similar to our states. The borders were open for us to cross without going through customs. They also have free trade between them.

Once in Portugal, the land became rockier, and the small farms clung to the hillsides. Cattle, goats, and sheep grazed in the pastures. The storks we had watched all through Spain didn't live in Portugal. It was noticeable how primitive farming was when we watched a farmer working in the field. A two-wheeled cart loaded with brush was being pulled from the field by a donkey.

In Fatima, we learned the story of the Basilica of Our Lady of the Rosary. It seems that in 1916, three children were watching their sheep in the field when they were visited by an angel. It had begun to rain, and the children had run for shelter. The clouds separated, and a light beamed from the sky to the earth. An angel appeared and asked the children to kneel and pray. The angel prayed the same prayer three times and then left. The children were so filled with God that they didn't speak all day, not even to each other. On May 13, 1917, the Virgin Mary appeared to them and told them to pray for peace. It took thirteen years for the courts to decide if this was a story or a miracle. In 1930, it was decided that the story was true. The basilica was built in honor of the Virgin Mary. A chapel was built where the children had stood. People come to pay homage, to be healed, or to ask for strength to deal with their problems. Many of them came from the parking lot walking on their knees. The children Jacinta and Francisco were brother and sister; they are buried at the basilica. Sister Louisa, a cousin, became a nun and was living at the convent. She was ninety-one years old at the time of our visit.

Lisbon hosted the World Expo in 1998, and when we were there, everyone was busy sprucing up the city. Two of my ladies, Martha and Grace, were beginning to wear out and needed to rest. They were taken to the hotel to lie down, and then the rest of the group visited the little fishing village of Cascais. The village began as a home to the fishermen, whose lives were confined to labor and the task of survival. Then it evolved into a resort center with four- and five-star hotels, sandy beaches, cafés, and souvenir stands. Many kings and important people have summer homes here.

Commandment number four of the Traveler's Ten Commandments states, "Remember thy passport so that thou knowest where it is at all times. For a man without a passport is a man without a country."

Grace discovered she had left her passport in the drawer of the bedside table in Salamanca. That was a nerve-jerker! The hotel was called, and then we waited. They had to go to the room and check to see if it was still in the drawer. It was! It was mailed and delivered to our hotel by Federal Express. It arrived the day before the group left Lisbon. Sometimes, I think my group is jinxed. At our rest stop in Montemaro, another lady in my group got locked in the restroom. After that, I stood outside the door and guarded so we didn't need to close the door all the way.

A highlight for me was a stop in a cork grove. I didn't even know cork grew on trees. I hadn't even thought about where cork came from before we stopped here. It is one of those things we take for granted; it is just there. A cork tree is an oak tree; the bark is the outer layer, and then comes the cork, then the Cambrian layer, which is the tree. Passing these cork groves, we would see numbers painted on them, such as an *8* or *9*. That was the year these trees were harvested. For instance, the trees with the *8* painted on them would be harvested in 1997, because they are harvested every nine years. We had permission to take free samples of cork off certain trees. It was a good thing I had my jackknife. Everyone was using it to peel off a sample of cork. After the cork is peeled from the trees, it is brought to factories, where it is boiled to soften it, and then it's flattened and dried. The cork is shipped to another factory, where corks are cut and the scraps are ground up to be made into sheets for wall boards, purses, and soles of shoes.

Returning to Spain, our group spent the night in Sevilla. As people were leaving the hotel and going out for an evening walk, shopping, or dinner, the desk clerks were stopping them and telling the ladies to bring their purses back to their rooms or put them in the safe. That was something we hadn't experienced before anywhere. We found out why before the night was over. Emily, who was with the group, was walking on the sidewalk with her friends when she felt someone grabbing the strap of her camera. She screamed and hung on for all she could, but the thief jerked it out of her hands, ran ahead, and jumped on the back of a motorcycle. They were gone, and so were her camera and all the pictures she had taken in Portugal. Emily spent the next morning at the police station.

To get to Africa, we took a forty-five-minute ferry ride from Spanish soil to Spanish soil. Then the coach took us across the border into Ceuta, Morocco, in northern Africa. Our guide collected our passports and took them to the customs officials. It took more than an hour. First, they needed to open each one and take out the form, and the passports were then passed to three different people. One of them dropped them all on the floor. Each name and passport number was entered into a computer. Since they couldn't type, it was a hunt-and-peck entry. Then each passport had to be stamped and stamped again with a special number entered in the book. That blurred! So they went over all the numbers in pen. Our guide was bringing the passports back to the coach ten at a time. He was afraid we wouldn't get them all, so he wanted to be sure we had them before the coach left the border. The newer passports were just stamped "Passport agency," with no town noted, and that was also confusing. We were entertained watching the people walking over the border from Spain with packages. Supplies were cheaper in Spain, so the women crossed the border to shop. They bought diapers, soap, and some groceries. They divided the packages to sell in their markets to make a dollar. The women we watched were like pack horses. Boxes and packages were tied in blankets and fastened on their backs and heads. The border patrol would shove, kick, and hit them; they were abusive to both men and women. I don't know what was going on, but sometimes one would give the patrol guard something (maybe money) so they wouldn't need to go behind the wooden screen and through the hassle of opening all their packages. From there, four or five people would get a taxi and ride into Ceuta, a city of seven hundred thousand people. Everything was finally taken care of for our group at the border; another guide joined us for the ride into Morocco and the continent of Africa. We noticed a number of cars abandoned at the border with numbers on the windshields. Our local guide explained that these had been confiscated for some reason or another. Maybe they were bringing something across the border they shouldn't. There was even a bus sitting there awaiting trial. Once trial is over, the vehicle can be moved. Another thing we noticed was that all the little boys on the street would smile and wave as the coach passed. Then it dawned on us that we were just seeing little boys; there were no little girls out playing. In fact, all the time we spent in Morocco, we did not see any little girls that weren't at the side of their mothers. Late afternoon, we entered the city of Tetauan. We had a walking tour through the streets to experience the city. Immediately, there were two more men that joined our group. One walked at each side, our local guide was leading, and the tour director and I were in the back of the group. Usually, when we had a local guide, our tour director was not with us, but we soon found out that Tetauan was full of hustlers and they were swarming all around. I knew then that we were being protected from purse-snatchers. The children were told to back away when they tried to mix in with the people. As we walked through the market, everything was being sold: clothing, vegetables, fruits, and even live chickens. At a trade school, we saw some wood latticework and carpet-weaving that the very young boys were doing. They were learning a skill to make a living. I had a feeling it was just the very lucky boys who could come to the trade school. All the while we walked, someone was popping up taking pictures. Was I surprised after leaving the city: we were a few miles out of town when this man came down the aisle with snapshots to sell! I couldn't believe he had boarded the coach.

The ride to Tangier was fascinating. I was glued to the window. All of the scenery, people, and lifestyle reminded me of biblical scenes that I've either seen in pictures or imagined. People working in the fields were shocking grain with all the work being done by hand. Burros were loaded with baskets, and we even saw a woman in a robe riding a burro sidesaddle. The wells were open stone wells by small, primitive homes. There were flocks of sheep and small herds of goats grazing wherever there was grass. Women sat in groups along the road selling goat cheese and baskets. Even our hotel in Tangier was very old, very unique, and picturesque. It is like staying in an antique. The belly dancer at our evening show embarrassed many in our group. She was overweight, her top hardly covered what it was supposed to, and she half-stripped one of the men in our group. He happened to be a doctor from Chicago. He had had heart surgery at one time; there was a long zipper scar on his chest. His son and wife were with him. The belly dancer dressed him in a bra and skirt and then dragged him out in the middle of the room to dance. He was a good sport about it, but what can you do? A man we called Rudy didn't even smile, and two other men wouldn't even watch. I didn't like it either because I'm a prude. Belly dancing can be artistic when it is tastefully done. Everyone enjoyed the father/son acrobatic act that followed; it was wonderful.

The next morning, on the way to the breakfast room, I walked across the floor to the balcony to look across the street at the beach. A large, red stain that looked like a large pool of blood was spread all over the sidewalk. I brushed it out of my mind; it couldn't be blood. Later, Lucy came and told me about it. She had walked over to look. People had been stepping in it, and footprints had spread it down the sidewalk. Our guide explained it away when he told us that many dogs ran loose; they were not neutered, so the police would shoot them. They were poor shots and would just end up wounding them. With the first pop of the gun and the yelp of the dog, the rest would run away. He figured that was what had happened.

After a walking tour of Tangier's narrow streets, we boarded a ferry for a two-hour ride across the Strait of Gibraltar. It was a very long walk when we got off the ferry. Grace had had problems with her legs, hips, and back since day two, but her friend Martha surprised me. She began having chest pains, became short of breath, and had a very pale complexion. We were a long way from the building, but she refused a wheelchair and nitro pills. She did let me carry her bag, and we walked very slowly. Martha said this happened all the time and that she was seeing a doctor when she got home.

I had thought the Rock of Gibraltar was a symbol for an insurance company. That day, we learned it was a British colony. Our coach was exchanged for two mini-buses. A bigger vehicle would not have been able to maneuver the mountain roads. Two colonies of monkeys roamed the island. They were used to people but still wild. Winston Churchill once said, "When there are no more apes on the island, the island will no longer be British." They always make sure to keep at least twenty-four monkeys on the island, maybe more. They are fed and cared for very well. Our driver had a favorite monkey who climbed through the side window and sat on the steering wheel to enjoy a treat.

Driving toward Toledo, we passed miles and miles of olive groves. Then, as the scenery became more hilly, we were traveling through miles and miles of grape fields. Soon, we arrived in La Mancha, Spain. "To Dream the Impossible Dream" was written about Don Quixote from La Mancha. He was all brains, with a big imagination; a very unrealistic man, tall and skinny. His servant was all stomach and mouth. He was always getting Don Quixote out of messes. La Mancha is where saffron is grown. It comes from the crocus plant. It is harvested at dawn. The two stamens are pulled out, and within thirty minutes, they must be dried or roasted. This gives a good flavor to soups or rice. It turns the rice yellow. First, you boil the water (they say in a shallow pan), add two or three stamens, put the rice in, and bake it in the oven till done. You can add things like peppers, shrimp, or nothing. It is very tasty.

Commandment number seven of the Traveler's Ten Commandments states, "Thou shalt not worry, for he that worrieth hath no pleasure." I worried! Once again, Martha and I lifted Grace off the bus. Once again,

Martha became breathless and pale and had to rest. Her heart was not pumping oxygen into her lungs. She really needed a doctor. Our flight home was smooth. I think it was because we had a woman pilot. Ha!

These were passed on to us by our guide on the tour! It makes sense, and you can use it anywhere.

Traveler's Ten Commandments

1. Thou shalt not expect to find things as thou hast them at home, for thou hast left thy home to find things different.
2. Thou shalt not take anything too seriously, for a carefree mind is the beginning of a vacation.
3. Thou shalt not let the other tourists get on thy nerves, for thou art paying out good money to have a good time.
4. Remember thy passport so that thou knowest where it is at all times, for a man without a passport is a man without a country.
5. Blessed is the person who can make change in any language, for he shall not be cheated.
6. Blessed is the person who can say "thank you" in any language, for it shall be worth more to another than any monetary tip.
7. Thou shalt not worry, for he that worrieth hath no pleasure.
8. Thou shalt not judge the people of a country by one person with whom thou hast had trouble.

9. Thou shalt when in Rome do somewhat as the Romans do. If in doubt, thou shalt use thy American common sense and friendliness.
10. Remember thou art a guest in every land, and he that treateth his host with respect shall be treated as an honored guest.

And

Thou shalt do as thy guide tells thee at all times!

Chapter 14

One of the most exciting moments for me was when our group was allowed to be at the Kennedy Space Center in Florida when the Columbia was being launched, February 22, 1996. Their mission was to release an Italian satellite that was connected to Columbia by a twelve-mile-long tether. They were conducting microgravity experiments. The mission was to last thirteen days and sixteen hours. This was the second time for this experiment; the first time they tried, in 1992, it failed. Now the system had been redesigned, and four of the original 1992 crew had volunteered to try again.

Our group had reservations to be at the space center for a tour on February 22. We got word that they had cancelled all tours and would not be open to the public. Because we had a contract and had made the reservation so far in advance, we had permission to visit the grounds. Although we were not allowed to take the bus tour out onto the site, we knew the Columbia was at the launchpad, the crew was inside, and countdown had started at 4:00 PM the previous day.

Our group kept busy visiting Spaceport Central, the galleries, the memorials, and the shops and viewing the films at IMAX. When it was getting close to launch time, people began to gather to watch the liftoff. The air was charged with tension and excitement. Over the intercom, you could hear the announcer giving commentary on the happenings that were taking place at the launchpad. They counted down the minutes and then the seconds. It was so quiet not even the birds chirped. When the launch took place at 3:18 PM, the ground under our feet shook, the boom was deafening, and then we saw the flaming, bright white light clear the trees. We watched as it lifted higher and higher into the sky. People cheered, people cried, and my heart felt like it was going to explode. It was one of the most emotional moments of my life. We watched until the light was a tiny speck; then everyone slowly walked to the coach for a ride back to our hotel.

Florida is a wonderful place to visit in the winter. It is the land of sunshine, and there is a 99.9 percent chance that it is warmer than Minnesota in February. Getting there is not always easy, as we have driven through snow and ice as far south as southern Indiana. The slush has built up thick on the windshield and then frozen. The driver has had to pull over many times just to remove the ice. Then there is black ice! You don't always see that, and it creates problems. In the afternoon of our first day on the road, we stopped at a fast food place in Wisconsin. Returning to the coach after our coffee break, Karen slipped and fell on black ice in the parking lot. I didn't see her fall, and she didn't say anything, but later at the hotel, she told me she thought she should see a doctor. I asked her why; she told me about her fall and said she thought her arm was broken. We went to the desk to find out where the nearest hospital was, and then the hotel shuttle brought her and her husband to the emergency room. Karen got a temporary cast and was told to see a doctor when we got to Orlando. The first day in Orlando, the group went to Universal Studios, and the driver took Karen and her husband to the hospital, where she got a permanent cast. She was a very good sport; they joined us later to enjoy an afternoon at the park.

Speaking of Universal Studios, an incident happened there a few years later while I was there with another group. It was a lesson for me, and I'll pass it on to you. If you're familiar with that theme park, you will know that you enter through a long corridor. You may ride on a moving walkway or walk alongside it. On this particular tour, we had a man, Joe, who had trouble walking, so we got him a wheelchair. He was wheeled all around the park. I think everyone should get a wheelchair, as you get to the head of the lines and usually have a front row seat at the attractions. Late afternoon, we were returning to the coach, and I offered to push him awhile. Walking down the corridor, I chose to take the moving walkway instead of walking alongside. It worked really well until we got to the end; then the front wheels turned sideways, and Joe was dumped out on the floor with the wheelchair on top of him. I don't know how I managed to jump over the wheelchair, but I did. I grabbed the chair and moved it to the side. People were coming behind us and jumping over Joe, who was still on the floor.

Another man hopped up and sat on the railing; he thought his weight stopped the sidewalk. I think it was the button I pushed at the end of the railing. The moral of this story is, do not push a wheelchair on a moving walkway.

Another thing that is not a good idea is to leave clothes in your room when you go home, unless you want to get rid of them. I've actually gone to Goodwill or a thrift store and bought secondhand clothes and, when I'm done wearing them, left them in the room. I learned that trick from a friend. You need to leave a note on them that says, "Please discard." Otherwise, your clothes will beat you home. The only time they don't beat you home is when it is something you want and just forgot. People have forgotten favorite slippers or a nightie hanging behind the bathroom door. Then we call the hotel and hope they haven't been thrown away yet and then have them sent home COD. Another thing that gets left is cell phone chargers. They are usually left in the electrical outlets. I'll tell you a secret. Just go to the hotel desk and ask if they have a charger for your phone. They'll bring out a shoebox full; there has got to be one in the box to fit your phone.

If people are staying in a hotel for two or three nights, they have a tendency to unpack their suitcases and put their clothes in the drawers. When you spread out like that, it's easy to forget items. One tour member went shopping before a tour, buying all new clothes. We arrived at a hotel where we would be staying for three nights. His wife unpacked and put the clothes away in the closet and drawers. It was time to leave, and she repacked, taking the clothes out of the closet and her drawers, leaving all of her husband's new clothes behind. When she got home, she discovered it and tried to call the hotel to retrieve them. After a week of getting nowhere, she called me at the office. I called the manager and explained what had happened, and she went to check. All the clothes were still in the drawer; even though the room had been rented out many times, no one had found them. They packaged them up and shipped them to the lady, hopefully before the husband found out they were missing.

Chapter 15

"Stormy Weather" is a song sung by Ella Fitzgerald, Lena Horne, Frank Sinatra, and many other artists: "Don't know why there's no sun up in the sky, stormy weather." The song is a love song comparing love to weather. However, the first line of the song drifts through my mind whenever the weather isn't cooperating. Believe me when I say we have had a couple of storm-related adventures.

The snowstorm I remember the most happened at the end of April, of all things. That should almost be spring, with tulips and daffodils poking through the dirt. It was snowing lightly when we left the bus garage that morning on our way to Branson, but certainly nothing to be alarmed about. The farther south we went, the heavier the snowfall. It was that wet, sticky stuff. About fifty miles into the trip, the office called and told us Highway 23 was closed. Since the storm was coming from the west, we decided if we could go east and then south, we could get ahead of it and drive out of the snow. It would have worked, but a few miles from Tracy, there was a semi in the ditch. When we drove into town, we were stopped; they weren't letting anyone out of town because of the weather. We were trapped! The coach was parked by a little café, and we hung out, waiting for the snow to quit and the wind to go down. It didn't happen. By late afternoon, we knew we had to find a place for the people to stay. Tracy is a little town with one small motel. There were a few rooms left, and we took them for the group. People didn't know each other, but they got acquainted really fast. If the room had two beds, we put two couples in the room. One room had three beds; with three single men on the coach, they got that room. We had run out of rooms. The police contacted the church, and some of the members stepped up, offering an extra bedroom for the people. Everyone had somewhere to stay except the driver and myself. I ended up going home with the police officer. They were very nice; I joined them for dinner and then ended up sleeping in their small son's room. The driver slept in the coach.

The storm quit during the night, and the next morning, the sun was out, making everything look bright and white. The driver picked me up first, and we drove around picking up people all around town. A minister traveling with the group grinned and told me he had really liked my hair last night. My hair was wet, straight, and plastered to my head. I told him to watch his mouth; I laughed, and he snickered. The company paid each of the families for their help and then bought the group breakfast at the café. Soon, we were on the road again.

The driver drove straight through to Branson, stopping only for meals and rest stops, with the company picking up the tab. It was late when we arrived in Branson, but through it all, the group only missed one show. On the way home, one of the tour members approached me, smiling, and told me he had only spent fifty cents on the whole tour. He had bought an ice cream cone at McDonald's. What a nice, understanding group of people.

Only one other time, snow caused a little problem for my group. Returning home from Texas, we ran into snow in Minnesota. It was snowing, drifting across the roads, and more than a little slick. We didn't even bring the group back to the bus garage, but took them on to Willmar. The people who lived in the city were brought to their homes, and the rest of the group was brought to the hotel. The coach would have had no problem getting to the bus garage, but the people would have had trouble getting home in the dark on snow-packed roads. The company didn't want anyone sliding into the ditch or having an accident. The following morning, was all of them were picked up again and taken to the bus garage to get their cars. Our tour ended up being a little longer, but everyone was safe. The company also picked up the hotel tab.

A spring storm in northeastern Wyoming was a little scary. It was May, and we were traveling to Rapid City, South Dakota. The group had been on a mystery tour to Colorado and was returning home. It was late afternoon, and the coach was quiet. People were napping; some were reading when we noticed the black clouds that were building in the west. Keeping an eye on them, we saw tails dropping and going up into the clouds again. Then we spotted the same type of clouds in front of the coach. The wind was picking up.

A small herd of about six to eight cows stood in a deep hollow by a culvert along side of the road. All the cows had their heads down except one. That one cow had its head up and seemed to be watching the weather. That seemed eerie to me, I've never noticed that behavior in cattle before, and I was raised in farming country.

Mike continued to drive toward Rapid City. We came up behind a pick-up camper just as a gust of wind took the roof off the camper and hurled it out into the field. The couple's belongings were flying out; the canvas sides were flapping in the wind. They pulled off to the side of the road. About the only thing they could do was to secure anything else that was loose. There was no way they would have been able to retrieve the roof. Later at the hotel, we heard a tornado had done damage to a school and other buildings in southwestern South Dakota. We felt lucky that we had come through that unscathed.

Once in a while, people on the tour get sick, and we deal with that, but when a driver gets sick, it is major. The California tour returns to Minnesota through Wyoming. The group had stayed overnight in Rawlins, Wyoming. The next morning, the driver was busy loading luggage when he looked at me and said, "You have a very sick driver." He had been up all night long with flu-like symptoms. He didn't look too hot, either. We left but didn't get too many miles down the road before he began throwing up. I grabbed a trash bag and held it under his chin, and when he finished, I twisted it shut and discarded it in the garbage. He drove another ten miles and pulled over, got out, and was sick again. We stopped one more time before reaching Laramie. It was coffee time for the group, and the driver took a nap. Leaving again, we got to the interstate, only to find the road was closed due to blowing and drifting snow. That was a miracle in disguise. The driver called the office, and they arranged for rooms for the group at the Comfort Inn. He stopped the bus and went right to bed. The baggage boys and I unloaded the luggage and got them into the rooms for the people. Then I walked next door to a restaurant and made lunch reservations for the group, compliments of Rustad's. It was nice having the afternoon free in Laramie. Many of us walked to the mall and shopped. Late afternoon, I brought the driver some soup and 7-Up. He was feeling much better. The next morning, he was just as good as new, and we once again were on our way home, only a half a day late. One other time, a driver got sick, but Chuck was tour director for that group; since he can drive, he did both jobs. The driver lay down in the back and rested.

Chapter 16

The voice of one of our very talented tour members sums it up with one of her poems. She has given me permission to add it to my book. This is the story of our Nova Scotia tour in a nutshell. However, it could very well apply to all of them.

It was June 14, 2001.
The Nova Scotia tour had just begun.
I was in Kerkhoven of all places,
looking around at a lot of new faces.

There were Vangie and Lloyd, and the red hats they wore
indicated to me that good times were in store.
Kenny and Laura, DeWayne and Toni
stuck close together, and that's no boloney!

There's Suzie, who giggles with a gleam in her eye,
and Delmore, who always has ice cream and pie.
From New London, it's Burton and his quiet wife Ella.
He seems like he is a nice kind of fella.

There's Pauline from Morris and her husband, Don.
She writes everything down and knows what's going
on.

It's Judy who tries to keep Ernie in line.
He grins while he recites *Evangeline.*
He knows his Norwegian and is trying to teach
a little to everyone who comes in his reach.

Sally loves to go walking while swinging her arms.
Her partner is Hazel with her quiet charms.
Now Darlene will tell you, as only she can,
that Henning was always one awesome man.

Ervin and Millie make a great pair, you know.
They're riding with interest wherever we go.

There's Darby and Ralph, father and son,
enjoying the sights since day number one.
They're with Sharon, all from South Dakota.
That's good! We can't all be from Minnesota.

Linda and Florence—sisters? *No way!*
But that is what I heard Linda say.
Inez always is happy, but watch out for Arne,
'Cause if you're not careful, he'll fill you with blarney.
Ernie took a picture of a scarecrow and Shirley,
but after he took it, he said, "Now I worry!
I'm afraid when I look at the picture, I might
forget if Shirley's on the left or the right."

This covers our tour group; we're all having fun,
but in this poem, I can't leave out anyone.

Which brings us to Alice, who keeps us in line,
and whatever happens, it always goes fine.
Chuck doesn't say much, just lets Alice say
whatever she wants to, in her own way.

She told us exactly where we should go
when the ferry "landed," but Chuck said, *"Oh no!*
Ferries don't land on the ground like a plane," he said.
"They dock, Alice!"—and he started shaking his head.

And don't ask Alice, "What day is it today?"
It will always be Sunday if she has her way.
Alice wears cool clothes and always looks nifty.
She certainly can't be a day over fifty!

When we came into Canada, we exchanged our money
for loonies and toonies that seem rather funny.

We all saw the bus roll back *up* Magnetic Hill.
If it weren't for the brakes, we could be backing up
still.
We love seeing lupines; some of us bought seed,
and quite a few on the bus had a lobster feed.

We learned how to tell boy and girl lobsters apart,
but I need to tell you this straight from my heart:
it's not so important if we know the difference, it's
true,
just so girl and boy lobsters remember who's who!

We enjoyed PEI and Anne of Green Gables.

We probably have souvenirs that could fill many tables.

We visited the museum of Alexander Graham Bell,
and from this visit, we could tell—
we could compare him to the Canadian money.
Some of his ideas were a little bit funny.

The weather was perfect as we rode on the ferry.
We "landed" in Maine, all rested and merry.
One day, the restaurant had a hundred-mile view.
We all stuffed our stomachs, but that's nothing new.
All the food was so good we all wanted to try it.
Next week, some of us will have to go on a diet.

We're heading toward home now, but Niagara calls.
One final attraction will be the great falls.
After that, on the road again, our clothes getting messy,
getting closer to Minnesota and closer to Jesse.

I want to say, "Thanks, Chuck! You and Alice are the best."
In all of your trips, you pass the test.
The tours you plan suit us just swell.
Just which one is best is too hard to tell.

But now, folks, as this journey ends,
I'm the one going home—with lots of new *friends!*

This last bit was an afterthought. Myrna e-mailed it July 1, 2001! I guess she thought it needed to be done!

I thought we were going home,
that I had come to the end of the poem.

Shirley and Myrna, after eating their dinner,
Went walking, hoping that would help us get thinner,
But something happened; now there's more to tell.
You've already heard about how Shirley fell.

But maybe it really was just by chance;
Shirley wanted a ride in an ambulance,
and since the motel was pretty far,
Myrna rode back there with a cop—in his car

to get Shirley's insurance card and her purse,
and was thinking, "Oh my! What could be worse?
Ooops that was an accident—sorry
If some of the group is outdoors at the end of this
ride,
They'll see me arrive with the police at my side!"

Oh well, everything worked out okay.
She got what she needed and was soon on her way.
Back to the hospital, didn't take too long,
where Shirley was waiting to find out what was
wrong.

It was then that they told her her left arm was
broken.
The sad part about it was no one was jokin'.
Alice came too; she walked and she walked,
and while Shirley got plastered, we talked and we
talked.

There's just one thing left that I'd like to mention.
I wrote the poem—Shirley got the attention.

Written by Myrna De Boer
Prinsburg, Minnesota

Conclusion

Nathan Hale was a captain in the Continental Army during the Revolutionary War. Just before being hanged by the British for spying in 1776, he said, "I regret that I have but one life to give for my country."

When I left Rustad's in October 2010, I could say, "I regret that I have but one life to manage tours."

The job I had didn't seem like work. I enjoyed every aspect of making the reservations, writing the brochures, and going on the coach. It was time for me to retire. My back was giving out for the second time. I spent more time in the office and less time on the road. It was hard to sit by a desk all day. It was also hard if I needed to move luggage around or lift a cooler out of the bay. The first few weeks at home were hard. I found that when you're used to getting up and going somewhere every morning, it is a lot different to get up to stay home. So I cleaned!

Over the years, I've said I was going to write a book and call it *Alice in Wanderland.* People have encouraged me to put the stories down on paper. So here it is! I hope you enjoy the book, and I hope I've not offended anyone. I plan on doing some traveling and spending my kids' inheritance. I love mysteries; maybe I'll try writing a mystery. But mostly, I hope to be a bigger part of my kids' life. Might as well drive them nuts!

CPSIA information can be obtained at www.ICGtesting.com
Printed in the USA
BVOW051109130911

271099BV00001B/1/P

9 781456 764371